Cinco de Mayo

by Lola M. Schaefer

Consulting Editor: Gail Saunders-Smith, Ph.D.

Consultant: Gregory S. Rodriguez, Assistant Professor
Mexican American Studies and Research Center
University of Arizona

Pebble Books

an imprint of Capstone Press
Mankato, Minnesota

Pebble Books are published by Capstone Press
151 Good Counsel Drive, P.O. Box 669, Mankato, Minnesota 56002
http://www.capstone-press.com

2 3 4 5 6 06 05 04 03 02 01

Library of Congress Cataloging-in-Publication Data
Schaefer, Lola M., 1950–
     Cinco de Mayo/by Lola M. Schaefer
     p. cm.—(Holidays and celebrations)
     Includes bibliographical references and index.
     Summary: Simple text and photographs explain the history of Cinco de Mayo,
the commemoration of the victory of the Mexican army over the French army on
May 5, 1862, and how it is celebrated.
     ISBN 0-7368-0661-X
     1. Cinco de Mayo (Mexican holiday)—History—Juvenile literature. 2. Cinco de
Mayo, Battle of, 1862—Juvenile literature. 3. Mexico—Social life and customs—
Juvenile literature. [1. Cinco de Mayo (Mexican holiday) 2. Holidays—Mexico.
3. Mexico—Social life and customs.] I. Title. II. Series.
F1233 .S28   2001
394.26972—dc21   00-024165

Note to Parents and Teachers

The Holidays and Celebrations series supports national social studies standards related to culture. This book describes Cinco de Mayo and illustrates how it is celebrated. The photographs support early readers in understanding the text. The repetition of words and phrases helps early readers learn new words. This book also introduces early readers to subject-specific vocabulary words, which are defined in the Words to Know section. Early readers may need assistance to read some words and to use the Table of Contents, Words to Know, Read More, Internet Sites, and Index/Word List sections of the book.

Table of Contents

May

S	M	T	W	T	F	S
	1	2	3	4	⑤	6
7	8	9	10	11	12	13
14	15	16	17	18	19	20
21	22	23	24	25	26	27
28	29	30	31			

4

Cinco de Mayo is celebrated on May 5. Cinco de Mayo means "fifth of May" in Spanish. Mexican Americans think about their Mexican history on Cinco de Mayo.

Cinco de Mayo is a national holiday in Mexico. People remember the Mexican victory over the French army on this day.

The French army attacked the Mexican city of Puebla on May 5, 1862. The French army was larger than the Mexican army.

The battle lasted only one day. The Mexican army fought hard. They won the Battle of Puebla.

12

Some people celebrate Cinco de Mayo with parades. They ride on floats and wear colorful clothes.

Some people celebrate
Cinco de Mayo
by dancing.

Some people celebrate
Cinco de Mayo
by singing.

18

Some people celebrate
Cinco de Mayo
by eating Mexican foods.

Children swing at piñatas
on Cinco de Mayo.
Candy falls when the
piñata breaks.

Words to Know

army—a large group of people trained to fight on land

float—a decorated truck or platform that is part of a parade

Mexican—of or belonging to Mexico

Mexican American—a person who lives in the United States who has Mexican ancestry; Cinco de Mayo celebrations have been popular with Mexican Americans since the 1900s.

national—having to do with a country as a whole

piñata—a hollow, decorated container filled with candy; a person wearing a blindfold tries to break a piñata with a stick.

Spanish—the language that is spoken in Spain, as well as Mexico and other Latin American countries; Spanish is the official language of Mexico.

Read More

MacMillan, Dianne M. *Mexican Independence Day and Cinco de Mayo.* Best Holiday Books. Springfield, N.J.: Enslow, 1997.

Urrutia, María Cristina. *Cinco de Mayo:Yesterday and Today.* Toronto: Groundwood Books, 1999.

Vázquez, Sarah. *Cinco de Mayo.* A World of Holidays. Austin, Texas: Raintree Steck-Vaughn, 1999.

Internet Sites

Cinco de Mayo
http://www.worldbook.com/fun/cinco/html/cinco.htm

History of Cinco de Mayo
http://www.cincodemayo.net/eng/history.htm

Mexican Holidays: Cinco de Mayo
http://www.mexonline.com/cinco.htm

Index/Word List

Word Count: 144
Early-Intervention Level: 17

Editorial Credits
Mari C. Schuh, editor; Heather Kindseth, designer; Kimberly Danger and
    Heidi Schoof, photo researchers

Photo Credits
Bob Daemmrich/Pictor, cover
Corbis, 8
Elliot Varner Smith, 12
H. Huntly Hersch, 20
Joe Viesti/The Viesti Collection, 14
Library of Congress, 10
Place Stock Photo, 4, 6, 16
Richard Cummins, 1
Unicorn Stock Photos/Jeff Greenberg, 18